Ideals Children's Books • Nashville, Tennessee
an imprint of Hambleton-Hill Publishing, Inc.

Published by Ideals Children's Books
An imprint of Hambleton-Hill Publishing, Inc.
Nashville, Tennessee 37218

Printed and bound in the United States of America

ISBN 1-57102-302-X

Graphic Design/Art Direction
John Laughlin

Photography
Scott Bonner

Blackstone Magik Enterprises, Inc.
Licensor

Williams-Bell & Associates, Inc.
Packager

AROUND THE HOUSE
MAGIC

The BLACKSTONE Family Magic Shoppe

By Gay Blackstone

Ideals Children's Books • Nashville, Tennessee
an imprint of Hambleton-Hill Publishing, Inc.

CONTENTS

As a youngster growing up, I often traveled with my father, who was America's leading magician from 1918 until he retired in 1963. Our summers were spent at our home on Blackstone Island in Colon, Michigan. The lack of air conditioning in theaters necessitated that we "take the summer off" and many idle days were spent refurbishing props and recharging our batteries. My early tricks and feats were always done with things found in the house, the hotel, or on our trips to the beach or the mountains. Using whatever was available, or whatever I was allowed to have from the barn where we kept the props, I created many tricks. These adventures from my mind became some of the amazing feats you'll find in this book.

—Harry Blackstone, Jr.

AROUND THE HOUSE
MAGIC

The Empty Glass

This simple trick will keep your friends guessing—
until you show them just how easy it is!

YOU NEED:
- 4 toothpicks
- a dime (or any other coin)
- a friend

Challenge a friend to take the dime out of the glass without touching it and by moving only two toothpicks. Here's how it's done.

1. Take four toothpicks and form a "glass." Then place the dime inside of it as shown below.

2. To perform this trick, simply slide the center toothpick to the left.

3. Bring the other toothpick over to re-form the glass. Mission accomplished!

Magic is simply a well-practiced trick.

Once you know the secret,
you can win this game every time!

YOU NEED:
- 30 toothpicks
- a friend

1. Ask a friend to play a game with you.

2. Make a pile of 30 toothpicks.

3. Explain that the two of you will take turns removing between one and six toothpicks at a time from the pile. The player to take the last toothpick will be the winner. (What you don't explain is that you are going to mentally keep a running total of all the toothpicks removed, and that you will make your moves equal the totals of 9, 16, and 23. When you make those moves, it is impossible for your friend to win!)

HERE'S A SAMPLE GAME:

1. Suppose your friend starts by taking out four toothpicks. To make it a total of nine toothpicks removed, you take away five.

2. Now he picks up three, making the total removed 12. So you take out four to get to 16, which is your second key number.

3. Maybe now he takes only two, so you grab five to bring the total to 23. Now he can't win, because no matter how many he takes you'll get the last one—the winning toothpick!

The most important rule of magic is:
Never reveal your secrets!

Four-Five-Six

*This game is as simple as checkers to learn,
but as hard as chess for your opponent to win.*

YOU NEED:
- 15 toothpicks
- a friend

1. Lay out three rows of toothpicks with four in the first row, five in the second, and six in the third.

2. Take turns with your opponent. On each turn, remove any number of toothpicks from any one row. You can take just one toothpick, the entire row, or any number in between.

3. The person to take the last toothpick loses.

4. Either player can start. After a few games, your opponent will be puzzled. There isn't any real pattern to your play, but you win almost every time.

The Secret

1. If you have the first move, you can be sure to win by removing only one toothpick from any row.

2. Regardless of who starts, make your moves so that your opponent is faced with the three rows making up one of the following patterns:
1-4-5   1-2-3   1-1-1
or two rows of equal numbers. If you remove enough toothpicks each time to leave one of these patterns, she will be forced to take the last one.

3. For example, let's say your opponent is looking at 1-1-1 and she takes the one in the first row. You take the one in the second row, which leaves her with the losing one in the third row.

*Never perform the same trick more than
once for the same audience.*

This trick is so easy—
your friends won't believe they fell for it!

YOU NEED:
- 3 empty glasses
- 3 glasses filled with water
- a friend

1. To begin this trick, put the glasses in a row so that the three full glasses are followed by the three empty glasses, as shown above.

2. Then say to your friend, *"Do you know that by moving only one glass I can have them alternate? That is, they'll be empty, full, empty, full, empty, full. Try it."*

3. When your friend has given up, simply pick up the second full glass *(Figure 1)*, pour its contents into the second empty glass, and then replace it. So easy—when you know the secret!

Figure 1

Mission accomplished!

A sleight of hand *is a secret movement of the hands that tricks the audience.*

CUT BUT UNCUT

Your audience—and the cup—will be left hanging!

YOU NEED:
- a strong piece of string or yarn
- a cup with a handle (be sure to ask a grownup which cup to use)
- scissors
- a friend

1. Have a friend hold one end of the string while you tie the cup to the other end.

2. Have her hold the string so that the cup dangles over the table.

3. Now say, *"I'll betcha I can cut that string, right in the center, but the cup won't fall. And no, I won't be holding the ends in my other hand."*

4. She will, of course, tell you that you can't possibly defy the laws of gravity like that, and she will ask you to prove it. Simply reach over and tie a knot in the center of the string, forming a loop.

5. Then cut the loop, leaving the knot in place. The string is cut, but the cup doesn't fall!

*Be calm, look your audience straight in the eye,
and speak clearly.*

Amaze your friends with a little bit of creative thinking.

YOU NEED:
- a magnet
- a paper clip
- a glass of water
- a friend

1. Drop a paper clip into a glass of water so that it rests near the side of the bottom of the glass. Say to your friend, *"I betcha you can't get the paper clip out of the glass without getting your fingers wet."* And don't let him use a pencil or put anything else inside the glass.

2. Once your friend has given up, take out a small magnet. Hold it against the outside of the glass near the paper clip.

3. Slowly pull the magnet up to the top of the glass. The paper clip will follow along on the inside (*Figures 1 & 2*).

Figure 1   *Figure 2*

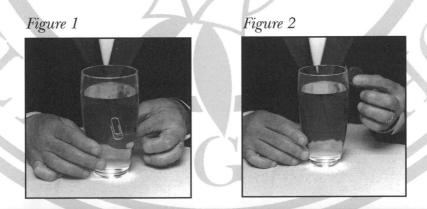

Patter *is what is said to distract an audience while a trick is being performed.*

Amaze your friends with this optical illusion.

YOU NEED:
- a piece of paper
- a pencil or pen
- a glass of water
- an audience

1. Draw a simple arrow on a piece of paper.

2. Show it to your audience and challenge anyone to change the direction of the arrow *without* turning the paper around or flipping it over.

3. The secret is to put the drawing behind a straight-sided glass full of water. The water will act as a lens and will make the arrow look as if it is going in the other direction.

At the beginning of any performance, always introduce yourself to the audience.

*Save this trick for a sunny day—in case
your friend gets soaked with water!*

YOU NEED:
- a glass of water
- a friend

1. Challenge a friend to pour a glass of water down his neck without getting his shirt wet. Usually you will be dared to do it first, which you gladly agree to do.

2. Simply pick up the glass and drink!

*Magic must be not only amazing,
but also interesting.*

Anything i Can do You

The basic idea of this trick is that your friend can't seem to copy your actions. Actually, it's impossible!

YOU NEED:
- 3 empty glasses
- a friend

Challenge a friend by saying,

"There are three empty glasses on the table. The middle one is turned opposite to the other two. By turning two glasses at a time, I can have them all upside down in just three moves. I'm going to do the trick once so that you know it can be done, but I betcha you can't do the same thing."

The Secret

1. When you do the trick, start with the first glass right side up, the middle glass upside down, and the third glass right side up.

2. Quickly turn over glasses 1 and 2 together (*Figure 1*), then 1 and 3 (*Figure 2*), and finally 1 and 2 again (*Figure 3*). Try crossing your wrists when you make the second move to further confuse your friend, but leave the glasses in their rightful places.

3. When it's your friend's turn, place the center glass right side up and the other two glasses upside down. It is now impossible for her to finish with all three glasses upside down in three moves. In other words, you can *only* finish with all three glasses in the same position that the middle one is in at the beginning.

Jean-Eugène Robert-Houdin is often referred to as the "father of modern magic."

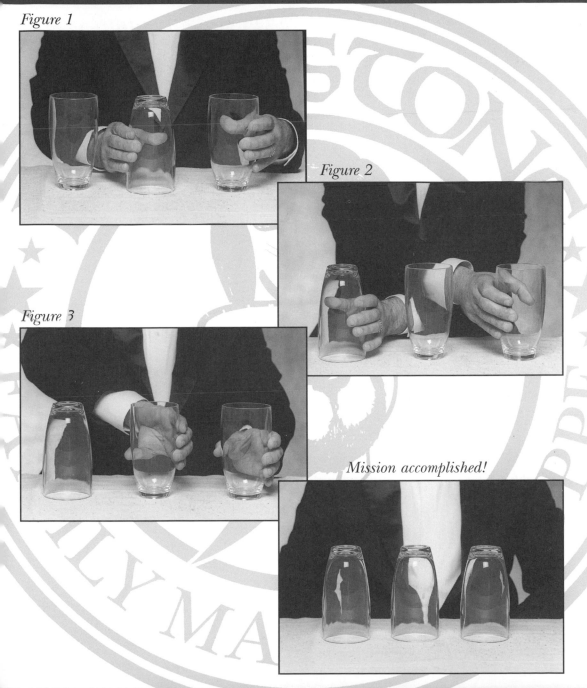

Figure 1

Figure 2

Figure 3

Mission accomplished!

Magicians in Europe and England are often called conjurers.

Here's the perfect way to prove that brains are mightier than muscles.

YOU NEED:
- a glass of water
- a friend

1. Put a glass of water in your right hand. Say to your friend, *"I don't think that you are strong enough to stop me from taking even one drink from this glass."*

2. When he is ready, have him hold your right wrist firmly with both hands. Perhaps he'd like to brace his feet on the floor in some way too. After all, you don't want to take unfair advantage. For a little added drama, let someone count to three so that you will both be prepared for the mighty effort.

3. When the moment arrives, simply reach over with your left hand, take the glass, and down a refreshing gulp.

In order for a magician to be successful, he must persuade the audience to like him.

Defy the laws of gravity!

YOU NEED:
- a glass of water
- a piece of cardboard

1. Say to a friend, *"I betcha I can hold water in an upside-down glass."*

2. Fill a glass to the brim with water.

3. Press a square piece of cardboard over the top of the glass to make a good seal.

4. Keeping the glass over the sink, very carefully and quickly turn it over. The water will stay inside, and the cardboard will stay sealed to the glass.

Using a magic wand *gives your performance a professional look.*

Put your head through a postcard!

YOU NEED:
- a postcard (or index card)
- scissors
- an audience

1. Say to your audience, *"I betcha I can cut a hole in a postcard that is big enough to put my head through. And I'll keep the card all in one piece!"*

2. Take a postcard (or an index card) and fold it in half across its width (*Figure 1*).

3. Using scissors, make a cut down the center of the card going from the folded edge to about 1/4 inch from the ends (*Figure 2*). Open the card and refold it, this time along the cut.

4. Beginning at one end of your long cut, make small cuts toward the outside edge. Place them a little more than 1/4 inch apart. Each cut should stop about 1/4 inch from the outside edge. Continue until you reach the other end of your long cut. You should get about ten cuts (*Figure 3*).

5. Turn the card around. In between each of your first cuts, make another cut from the outside edge toward the center (as in *Figure 3*, only from the opposite side). Each cut should stop 1/4 inch from the long cut running down the center of the card.

6. When you've finished, carefully open the card (*Figure 4*).

7. Crease each of the joints flat (*Figure 5*). Now you have a paper ring about 45 inches around that will easily slip over your head.

A magic scholar is a person who studies the history of the art of magic.

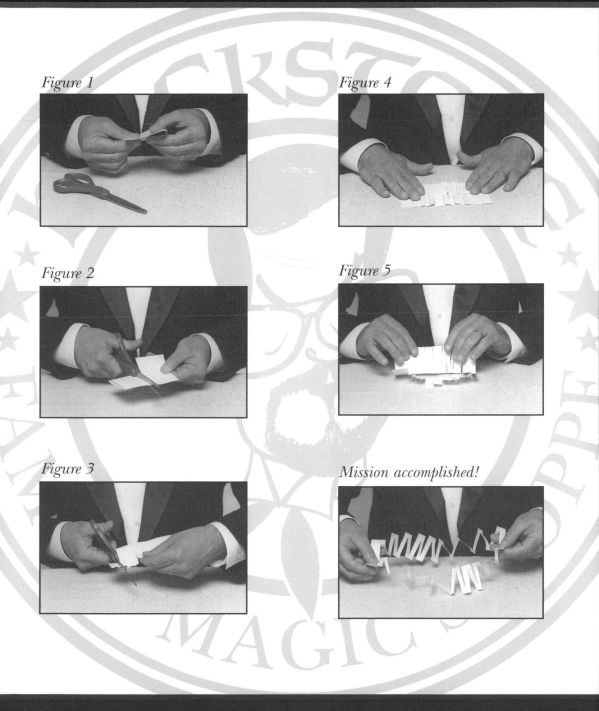

Figure 1

Figure 4

Figure 2

Figure 5

Figure 3

Mission accomplished!

Magicians were so honored by the Greeks that statues were erected of famous magicians such as Euclides, Zenaphon, and Theodorus.

Prove that you have the steadier hand.

YOU NEED:
- a cork
- a glass
- a pitcher of water
- a friend

1. Say to a friend, *"I betcha my hand is steadier than yours."* When she asks for proof, do the following:

2. Fill a glass almost to the top with water.

3. Drop a cork into the glass.

4. Tell your friend to hold the glass in one hand and make the cork stay in the center. But no matter how steady she tries to be, the cork will float to the side and stick to the glass (*Figure 1*).

Jacob Meyer was the first magician born in North America. For his stage name, he took the name of his birthplace and so became Jacob Philadelphia.

The Secret

To prove that your hand is the steadier hand, do the following:

1. Take the pitcher of water and gently pour water into the same glass containing the cork (*Figure 2*).

2. Keep pouring until the surface of the water is slightly above the rim of the glass, but be careful not to overflow the water! The cork will float to the highest point—the center of the glass (*Figure 3*).

3. Very gently pick up the glass and, to everyone's surprise but yours, you've won!

Figure 1   *Figure 2*

Figure 3

P.T. Selbit, an Englishman, created the illusion
of sawing a woman in half.

Tie a handkerchief in a knot—while holding both ends!

YOU NEED:
- a handkerchief or scarf
- a friend

Figure 1

1. Hold one corner of a handkerchief in each hand. Now say to a friend, *"I betcha I can tie a knot in this handkerchief without ever letting go of the ends."*

2. Offer to let her try it first. If she is willing to give it a try, put the handkerchief in her hands (*Figure 1*).

3. When she declares that it is an impossible task, take the handkerchief and drop it on the table.

4. Cross your arms.

5. Lean down and take one end of the handkerchief in one hand, then lean in the opposite direction so that your other hand can pick up the opposite corner (*Figure 2*).

5. Carefully unfold your arms and reveal your prize-winning knot (*Figures 3 through 5*)!

Harry Blackstone, Sr. changed his name from Harry Bouton after seeing a box of Blackstone cigars.

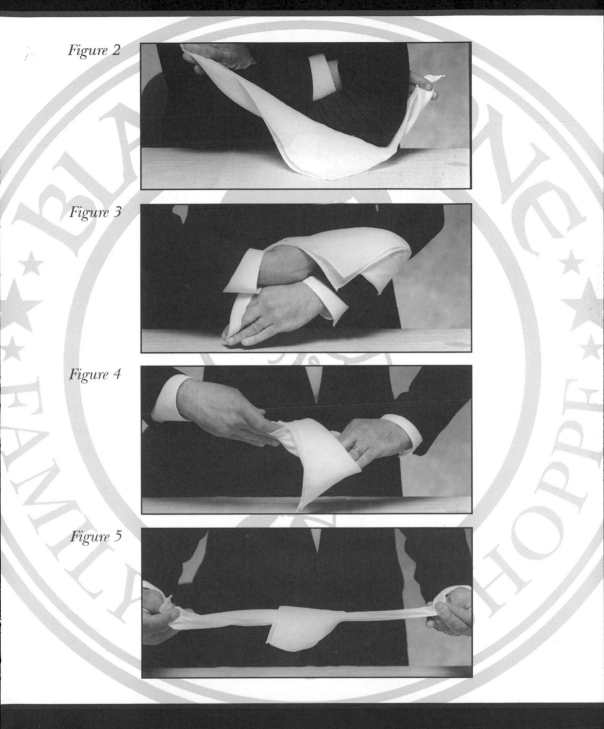

Figure 2

Figure 3

Figure 4

Figure 5

When an object magically appears it is referred to as a production.

LEFT VS. RIGHT

This trick is so simple, it gets them every time!

YOU NEED:
- a friend

1. Say to a friend, *"I betcha I can put something in your left hand that you can't hold in your right hand."*

2. When the challenge has been accepted, simply cup his right elbow in his left hand. End of trick!

BODY SPELLING

Challenge your friend's knowledge.

YOU NEED:
- a friend

1. Say to a friend, *"I betcha you can't name ten parts of the body that are spelled with only three letters. I'll give you one minute to do it."*

2. Unless your friend is a doctor, this will be an almost impossible task. And don't let him get a running start to ten with any answers like, "Five toes and two eyes make seven."

The answers:

Arm, ear, eye, fat, hip, jaw, leg, lip, rib, toe

An illusion uses astounding props such as large animals and people.

The Weakest Link

A chain is not supposed to be stronger than its weakest link, and if the weakest link is nothing more than ordinary thread, how strong can the chain be?

YOU NEED:
- a spool of thread
- a friend

1. Say to a friend, *"I betcha I can tie you up with a piece of ordinary thread so that you can't move."*

2. Remove a spool of thread from your pocket and show him how easy it is for you to break the thread between your hands. Of course, he'll think it's impossible to be tied up with a simple piece of thread.

3. When he accepts your challenge, ask him to sit on the floor and cross his legs.

4. Have him put his arms between his legs and around his ankles.

5. Tie his thumbs together by looping the thread around his thumbs several times. He'll soon discover that it's one thing to break a thread between his hands and another to break it between his thumbs.

A trick uses smaller objects such as cards or coins.

In this trick you'll prove the hand is quicker than the eye!

YOU NEED:
- 2 dice
- a small glass
- an audience

1. With your audience watching, wrap your middle finger and thumb around a glass and hold a die between them (*Figure 1*).

2. Stack a second die on top of the first one (*Figure 2*).

3. Give a little toss and catch the second die in the glass (*Figure 3*).

4. Repeat the procedure and catch the other die in the glass.

5. Now offer to let someone from the audience try it.

The funny thing is that every time someone else tries it, she may get one die into the glass, but will lose the second one.

The Secret

Maybe what your audience didn't notice is that you really didn't toss the second die up into the air. Actually, you just let go of the die and dropped the glass under it so that it *fell* into the glass with the first die (*Figures 4 through 6*).

Dice *are great props to use because they are easily carried—perfect for a sleight-of-hand trick!*

Figure 1

Figure 4

Figure 2

Figure 5

Figure 3

Figure 6

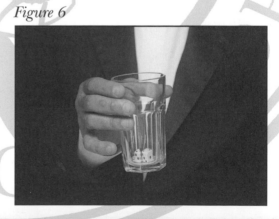

Transposition *is when one object changes into another.*

This test of strength will be no problem . . . for you!

YOU NEED:
- 2 paper napkins
- a glass of water
- a friend

1. Take two paper napkins, and open them out flat.

2. Twist each one individually into a tight rope shape (*Figure 1*).

3. Then say, *"I betcha you can't tear one of these little napkins in half."*

4. If he challenges you to try it first, then gladly accept.

5. Before you reach for the twisted napkin, secretly wet the tips of both thumbs. (You can do this by accidentally spilling a little water on the table or by moving your thumbs over the outside of a "sweaty" glass.)

6. When you pick up the napkin with your fingers, touch your thumbtips to the center of the napkin (*Figure 2*). The moisture will soak into the paper and weaken it just enough so that you're able to tear the napkin easily.

Restoration *is when something is destroyed*
and then is put back together again.

Figure 1

Figure 2

Mission accomplished!

Animation *is making inaminate objects move,*
such as a dancing handkerchief.

Your hair will seem as strong as a metal chain!

YOU NEED:
- a glass of ice water
- salt
- a hair from your head
- an audience

1. Tell your friends that not only is your hair strong, but that it must be magnetic because it can attract and hold heavy objects. Say to a friend, *"I'll prove this by lifting an ice cube out of this glass of water by using a hair from my head."*

2. Lay the center of the hair across the top of an ice cube.

3. Sprinkle salt over it (*Figure 1*).

4. Wait about a minute, then gently lift the two ends of the hair. The cube will come right out of the glass (*Figure 2*).

Penetration *occurs when one solid object passes through another solid object.*

The Secret

The salt melted the surface of the ice, but the cold of the ice cube refroze it, this time around the center of the hair.

Figure 1

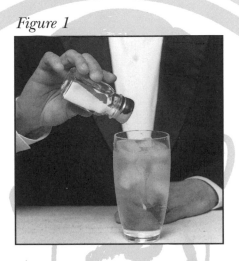

Figure 2

Suspension *is when an object is placed in the air and stays there, defying gravity.*

SALT AND PEPPER

Separate pepper from a pile of salt in the blink of an eye!

YOU NEED:
- salt
- pepper
- a plastic comb
- an audience

1. While your audience is watching, pour a small pile of salt in the center of the table and a larger pile a few inches away from it (*Figure 1*).

2. Pick up the pepper shaker, and add pepper to both piles (*Figure 2*).

3. As you mix each pile, look at your audience and say, *"I betcha I can separate salt and pepper faster than anyone else. In fact, I am so sure of it that you can even pick which pile I'll work with."* (Inevitably you'll get the larger pile, but don't worry about a thing. You can even add a little extra pepper just to show off.)

4. Take out a plastic comb and run it through your hair a few times.

Levitation occurs when an object rises into the air and is able to remain there without any physical support.

5. Wave the comb closely over the top of the pile (*Figure 3*). The pepper flakes will jump out of the pile and stick to it.

6. Wipe off the pepper flakes and repeat the process until the static electricity in the comb has removed all the pepper!

Figure 1

Figure 2

Figure 3

An illusion is a false perception of what one actually sees.

EGGS ON EDGE

Amaze your friends with this astonishing balancing act!

YOU NEED:
- an egg
- salt
- a table covered with a tablecloth
- an audience

1. Tell your audience that you can balance an egg on its end on the table.

2. Take a salt shaker and sprinkle a little pile of salt on the tablecloth.

3. Place the egg on the pile and firmly, but gently, settle it down, balancing it on the larger end (*Figure 1*).

4. Carefully blow away almost all the salt grains. The egg is balanced!

Positive illusions *occur when the audience sees something that does not exist.*

Figure 1

Mission accomplished!

Now, for something a little harder, tell your friends that you can balance the egg even without the salt!

1. Hold an egg with the larger end at the bottom.

2. Very gently hit the bottom end against the tabletop until a little bit of the shell breaks.

3. Balance the egg on this broken end. The egg will stand all by itself!

The Secret

The large end of the egg has a little air sac inside the shell. Hit the eggshell just hard enough to break the shell, but not hard enough to break the air sac.

Negative illusions *occur when the audience does not see something that does exist.*

An Egg Float

Float an egg in the middle of a glass of water!

YOU NEED:
- an empty glass
- a pitcher of water
- an egg
- salt
- a spoon
- an audience

Tell your audience that you can float anything if you really want to. In fact, you'll prove it with this simple demonstration.

1. Take an empty glass and fill it halfway with water.

2. Add salt and stir the water until the salt dissolves (*Figure 1*).

3. Continue to add more salt, stirring until the water can't dissolve any more salt (*Figure 2*).

4. Put an egg on a spoon and gently lower it down on the surface of the water (*Figure 3*). Eureka, it floats (*Figure 4*)!

An example of a natural illusion *is a pencil that appears to be bent when it is submerged in a glass of water.*

Figure 1   Figure 2   Figure 3   Figure 4

Make the trick even more astounding by doing the following:

5. Say to your audience, *"You think that's good? While you were watching me stir the salt into the water, I taught this egg how to swim underwater. What do I mean? I mean that if I add more water, the egg will stay in the middle of the glass."*

6. Gently add fresh water until the glass is full (*Figure 5*). The egg will float in the center of the glass, neither rising nor falling (*Figure 6*).

The Secret

The water and salt solution is heavier than the egg, so the egg floats on top of the salty water. But the egg is heavier than fresh water, so the egg stays at the bottom of it.

Figure 5   Figure 6

Magicians control what the audience thinks it sees by the use of misdirection; *that is, making the audience look at the wrong thing at the right time.*

STRONG FINGERS

Make your fists impossible to separate.

YOU NEED:
- a friend

1. Have a friend close each fist and place one on top of the other.

2. Using only the index finger of each hand and just tapping your friend's fists, you can easily separate her hands. When you switch positions, however, and she tries to do the same to your fists, she finds she cannot.

Figure 1

Figure 2

The Secret

3. When you hit her fists with your fingers, aim for her knuckles and strike them away from each other.

4. Now when you close your own fists and put them together, secretly slide your lower thumb up into your other fist (*Figure 1*). Your hands are now as hard to move as two boulders (*Figure 2*)!

Become an expert at doing a few solid tricks.
These will carry your performance.

No one can pull this one off.

YOU NEED:
- a piece of paper
- a friend

1. Make two tears in a strip of paper—one on each end, being sure not to tear all the way across the paper.

2. Say to a friend, *"I betcha that by holding one end in each hand, you can't tear both ends of this paper off in one pull."*

The Secret

Of course he can't, it's impossible. Remember, a chain is only as strong as its weakest link.

In magic, presentation is everything.

FIVE-FINGER LIFT

Amaze your friends with the laws of physics.

YOU NEED:
- an armless chair
- 5 friends

Say to a friend, *"I betcha I can lift you with just five fingers."* Watch the slow smile of delight come over your friend's face as she thinks of you trying to lift her using only five fingers. Is she in for a surprise!

1. Have your friend sit in an armless chair with her arms crossed.

2. You and four friends are now going to lift her out of the chair using just one finger each.

3. The first person puts a forefinger under the instep of her left shoe.

4. The second person does the same with her right shoe.

5. The third person hooks his finger around the bone just in front of your friend's left elbow.

6. The fourth person takes the same position at her right elbow.

7. Finally, you put your index finger crosswise under her chin so that you support both sides of her jawbone.

8. As you count to three the person in the chair is to lock her joints so that she becomes a solid object, but without stiffening her muscles. She is merely to prevent her knees and other body hinges from bending. At the same time you and the other four are taking a deep breath.

9. On the count of three, you all hold your breath and lift. Up will come your friend.

Utilize the laws of nature (for example, gravity) to aid you in your performance.

A Simple Tear

*Challenge your friend's strength with a
single sheet of newspaper.*

YOU NEED:
- a sheet of newspaper
- a friend

1. Ask a friend if he can tear a sheet of newspaper in half. Of course he will say yes. Then really challenge his strength by saying, *"Well, maybe you can tear a newspaper in half once, but I betcha you can't put the two halves together, tear it again, put the halves together, and tear it again—I betcha you can't tear it nine times."* This task will seem easy to your friend, until he tries it!

2. Give him a double-page spread of newspaper. Or, if you want to make the challenge even more difficult, give him a single page.

3. In either case, he won't get past the eighth tear. After all that tearing he will have 256 layers of 2-inch-square newspaper! There's no way he can keep them together to tear . . . even if he had the strength!

*It is more important to do a few tricks well
than to do many tricks.*

Step and Kick

You'll roll with laughter as you watch people try this stunt.

YOU NEED:
- a broom
- a friend

You'll need to go outside for this trick. (Try to find some soft, thick grass in case someone falls.)

1. First, cross your right leg behind your left leg.

2. Place the end of a broom handle on your right toes.

3. Take one step with your left foot and then kick the broom across the yard with your right foot.

With a little practice you can kick the broom quite a distance and, at the same time, make it look very simple. Some of your friends will find it difficult to get into the correct position. Others will get a surprise by kicking their left foot right out from under themselves.

The Secret

When you practice this trick, bend your left knee slightly as you kick with your right foot.

Magicians take simple events and make them happen in an unexpected way.

The Emergency Egg-Xit

Pull out this trick when you need
to make a clean getaway.

YOU NEED:
- a door
- an egg
- a friend

1. Ask a friend if she thinks she has strong, steady fingers. When she says yes, then offer this little test. Say, *"I betcha you can't put your first two fingers through the crack of a door, where the hinges are, and hold an egg without breaking the shell."*

2. As you are putting her behind the door, have her take off her shoes so that she doesn't slip in the narrow space.

3. When she has her fingers through the crack of the door, put an egg in her two fingers.

4. Then put her shoes under the egg and leave.

Your friend can't escape without dropping the egg into her own shoe!

Practice a trick until you are perfectly
at ease performing it.

A New Word

There's more than one way to make a new word!

YOU NEED:
- a piece of paper
- a pen or pencil
- a friend

1. Write the words "new door" on a piece of paper (*Figures 1 & 2*).

2. Give the paper to a friend and say, *"I'll betcha that you can't take the letters in the words "new door" and rearrange them to make one word out of them."*

3. Let your friend study the letters and try to complete the task.

4. When he gives up, take the paper and write "one word" (*Figure 3*).

Deciding the time and place for performing a trick is an extremely important part of stunning your audience.

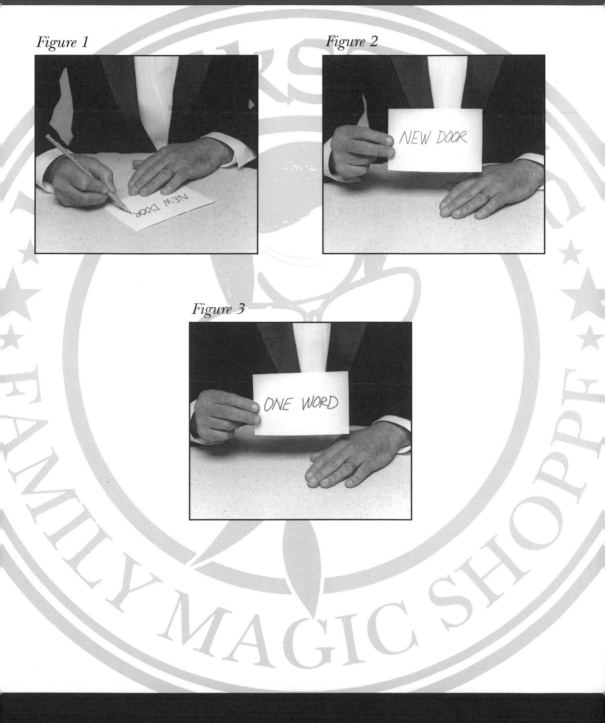

Figure 1

Figure 2

Figure 3

Find a way to work your tricks into a joke you know.
You can even create a new story to
embellish your trick.

This book is dedicated
to the memory of
Harry Blackstone, Jr.
1934 – 1997